FULL SCORE
WSB-10-005

吹奏楽譜 ブラスロック・シリーズ

BRASS ROCK

Get It On ～黒い炎～

作曲：Bill Chase　編曲：郷間幹男

楽器編成表

Piccolo	B♭ Trumpet 1	Drums
Flutes 1（& *2）	B♭ Trumpet 2	Timpani
*Oboe	*B♭ Trumpet 3	Percussion 1
*Bassoon	F Horns 1（& *2）	...Conga, Tambourine
*E♭ Clarinet	F Horns 3（& *4）	Percussion 2
B♭ Clarinet 1	Trombone 1	...Triangle, Wind Chime,
B♭ Clarinet 2	Trombone 2	Sus.Cymbal
*B♭ Clarinet 3	*Trombone 3	Mallet
*Alto Clarinet	Euphonium	...Glockenspiel, Xylophone
Bass Clarinet	Tuba	
Alto Saxophone 1	Electric Bass	
*Alto Saxophone 2	（String Bass）	Full Score
Tenor Saxophone		
Baritone Saxophone		

＊イタリック表記の楽譜はオプション

Get It On - 2

Get It On - 3

Get It On - 16

Get It On - 17

ご注文について

ウィンズスコアの商品は全国の楽器店、ならびに書店にてお求めになれますが、店頭でのご購入が困難な場合、当社PC&モバイルサイト・FAX・電話からのご注文で、直接ご購入が可能です。

◎当社PCサイトでのご注文方法

http://www.winds-score.com

上記のURLへアクセスし、WEBショップにてご注文ください。

◎FAXでのご注文方法

FAX.03-6809-0594

24時間、ご注文を承ります。当社サイトよりFAXご注文用紙をダウンロードし、印刷、ご記入の上ご送信ください。

◎お電話でのご注文方法

TEL.0120-713-771

営業時間内に電話いただければ、電話にてご注文を承ります。

◎モバイルサイトでのご注文方法

右のQRコードを読み取ってアクセスいただくか、URLを直接ご入力ください。

※この出版物の全部または一部を権利者に無断で複製(コピー)することは、著作権の侵害にあたり、著作権法により罰せられます。

※造本には十分注意しておりますが、万一、落丁・乱丁などの不良品がありましたらお取り替えいたします。また、ご意見・ご感想もホームページより受け付けておりますので、お気軽にお問い合わせください。

Piccolo

Get It On
~黒い炎~

Comp. by Bill Chase
Arr. by Mikio Gohma

Oboe
(Option)

Get It On
~黒い炎~

Comp. by Bill Chase
Arr. by Mikio Gohma

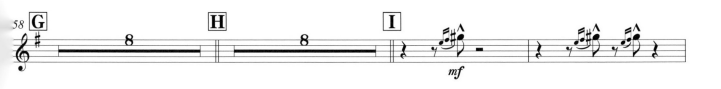

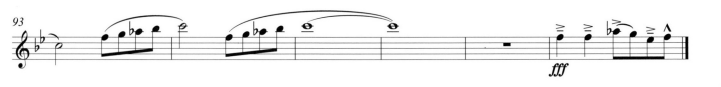

Tenor Saxophone

Get It On
~黒い炎~

Comp. by Bill Chase
Arr. by Mikio Gohma

Get It On
~黒い炎~

Baritone Saxophone

Comp. by Bill Chase
Arr. by Mikio Gohma

Get It On
~黒い炎~

B♭ Trumpet 1

Comp. by Bill Chase
Arr. by Mikio Gohma

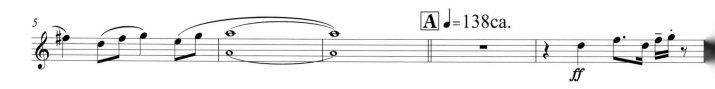

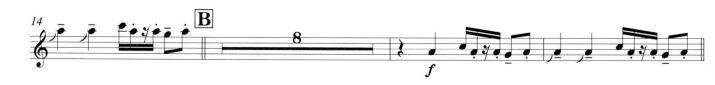

B♭ Trumpet 2

Get It On
~黒い炎~

Comp. by Bill Chase
Arr. by Mikio Gohma

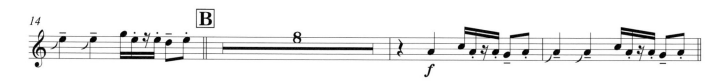

F Horns 1(&2)

Get It On
～黒い炎～

Comp. by Bill Chase
Arr. by Mikio Gohma

Horns 1(&2) — Get It On - 2

F Horns 3(&4)

Get It On
~黒い炎~

Comp. by Bill Chase
Arr. by Mikio Gohma

Trombone 1

Get It On
~黒い炎~

Comp. by Bill Chase
Arr. by Mikio Gohma

Trombone 2

Get It On
~黒い炎~

Comp. by Bill Chase
Arr. by Mikio Gohma

Euphonium

Get It On
~黒い炎~

Comp. by Bill Chase
Arr. by Mikio Gohma

Drums

Get It On
~黒い炎~

Comp. by Bill Chase
Arr. by Mikio Gohma

Electric Bass Guitar
(String Bass)

Get It On
~黒い炎~

Comp. by Bill Chase
Arr. by Mikio Gohma

Timpani

Get It On
~黒い炎~

Comp. by Bill Chase
Arr. by Mikio Gohma

Percussion 1
(Conga, Tambourine)

Get It On
～黒い炎～

Comp. by Bill Chase
Arr. by Mikio Gohma

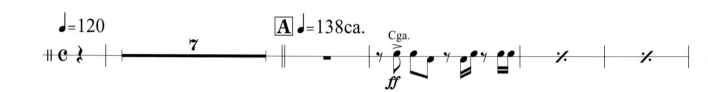
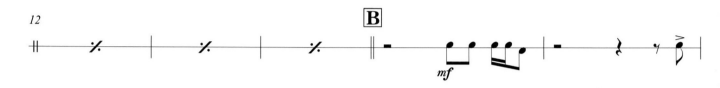

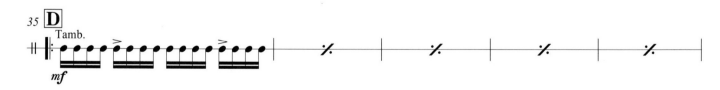
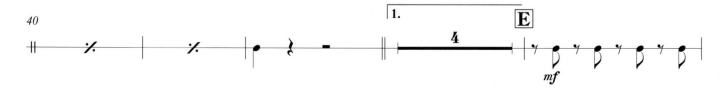

Percussion 1
(Conga, Tambourine)

Get It On - 2

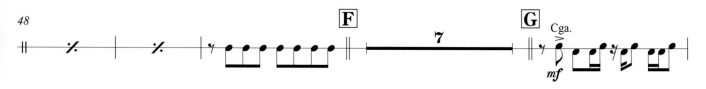
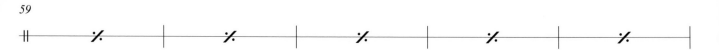
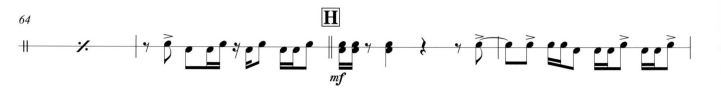

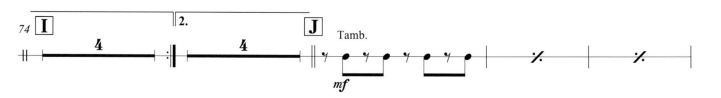
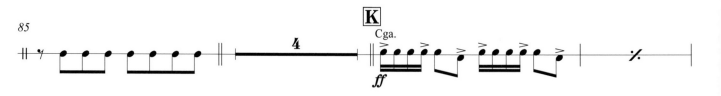
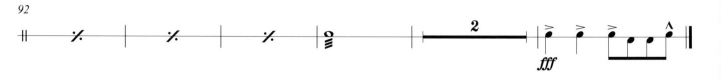

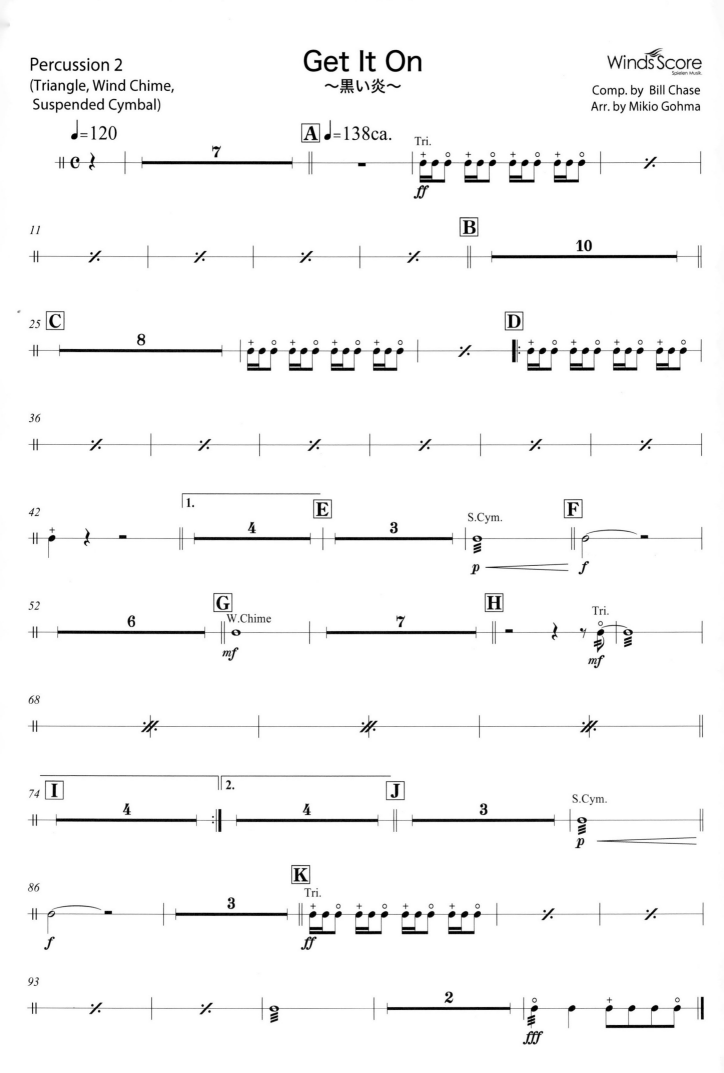

Mallet
(Glockenspiel, Xylophone)

Get It On
~黒い炎~

Comp. by Bill Chase
Arr. by Mikio Gohma

Mallet
(Glockenspiel, Xylophone)

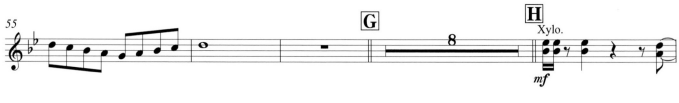